# Learning About Life Cycles

## The Life Cycle of a

# Crab

**Ruth Thomson**

**PowerKiDS** press.

New York

Published in 2009 by The Rosen Publishing Group Inc.
29 East 21st Street, New York, NY 10010

First Edition

Editor: Victoria Brooker
Designer: Simon Morse
Consultant: Michael Scott OBE, B.Sc

Library of Congress Cataloging-in-Publication Data

Thomson, Ruth, 1949-
   The life cycle of a crab / Ruth Thomson. — 1st ed.
      p. cm. — (Learning about life cycles)
   Includes index.
   ISBN 978-1-4358-2834-6 (library binding)
   ISBN 978-1-4358-2884-1 (paperback)
   ISBN 978-1-4358-2890-2 (6-pack)
   1. Crabs—Life cycles—Juvenile literature.
   I. Title.
   QL444.M33T46 2009
   595.3'86—dc22

                                   2008026175


Manufactured in China

Photographs: 14 Frank Greenaway/DK/Getty
Images; cover (cr), 13, 23br Image Quest 3-
D/NHPA; 6 Dave King/DK/Getty Images; 17
Frank Lane Picture Agency/Corbis; 21 Renee
Morris/Alamy; 12 Papilio/Alamy; 8 Steve
Stone/iStockphoto; 7, 19 Roy Waller/NHPA; 1, 2,
4, 7, 9, 10, 11, 15, 16, 18, 20, 22, 23tr, 23tl, 23bl
naturepl.com

## Web Sites

Due to the changing nature of
Internet links, PowerKids Press has
developed an online list of Web sites
related to the subject of this book.
This site is updated regularly.
Please use this link to access this list:
www.powerkidslinks.com/lalc/crab

# Contents

# Crabs live here

Crabs usually live in the sea, by sandy or rocky seashores. They hide during the day. At night, they come out to feed.

# What is a crab?

A crab has a soft body, which is protected by a hard, shiny shell. It has five pairs of **jointed** legs. The front two legs have claws. The others are used for walking and swimming.

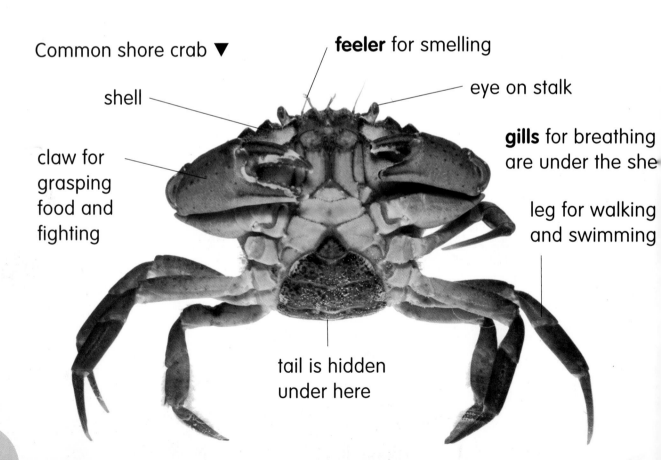

Common shore crab ▼

**feeler** for smelling

shell

eye on stalk

**gills** for breathing are under the she

claw for grasping food and fighting

leg for walking and swimming

tail is hidden under here

The crab's dark, blotchy shell is almost the same color as the rocks where it lives. This makes it hard to see.

# Finding a mate

In the summer, a male crab finds a female to **mate** with.

eggs

The female lays thousands of tiny eggs.
She carries them around tucked under her
tail. They are attached to stiff **bristles**.

# Larvae

When the eggs are ready to **hatch**, the mother sits in the water and uncurls her tail. The eggs then float away.

**4 months**

he eggs hatch into tiny **larvae** with long spines that help them float. The sea carries them to new homes. Many larvae are eaten by fish and jellyfish on the way.

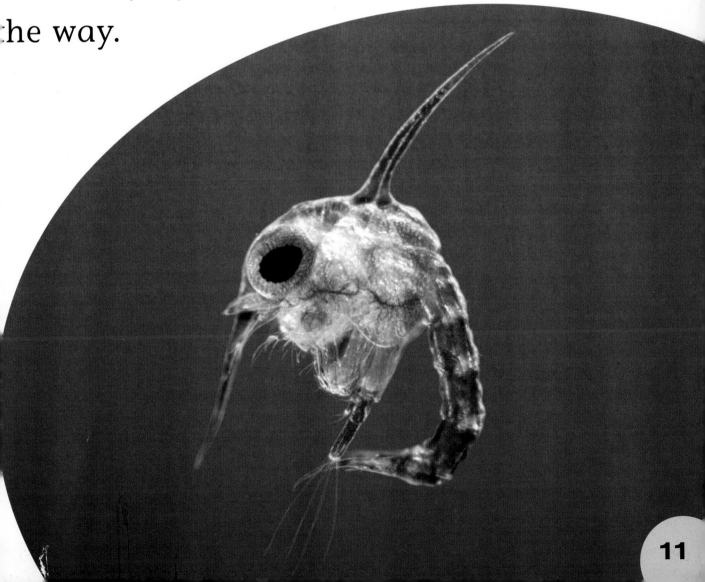

5 months

# Molting

A **larva's** skin cannot stretch.
As its body grows, the larva's skin splits
and falls off. This is called **molting**.
It has a new skin underneath.

The larva molts several times. It changes shape and becomes a small crab. It grows too heavy to float, and sinks to the seabed.

# Feeding

A crab feeds on shellfish, such as mussels and clams. It crushes their shells with one claw and scoops out the inside with the other.

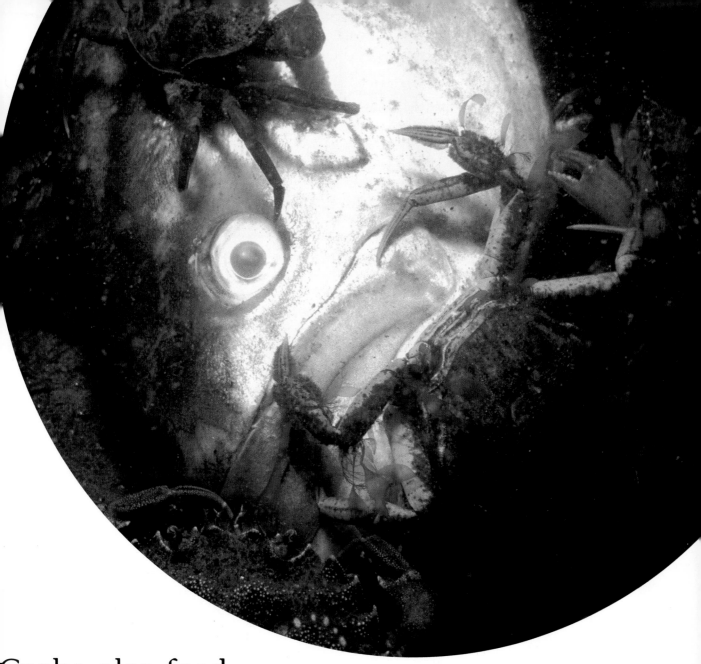

Crabs also feed
on dead animals, such as fish,
starfish, and other crabs.

# New shells

A crab keeps growing for several years. Its shell cannot stretch. As its body grows, the crab **molts** and grows a new shell.

old shell

new shell

At first, this new shell is soft.
The crab's body swells before the
shell hardens. The crab hides away
until the shell is completely hard.

# Dangers

Many crabs do not live very long.
They are eaten by all kinds of
birds, such as seagulls, herons,
and cormorants.

Eels, squid, dogfish, and big crabs that roam large rockpools also eat small crabs.

# Defenses

A crab waves its claws to **defend** itself from attack by crabs and other animals. It spreads its legs wide to look bigger and fiercer than it really is.

If a crab loses a claw in a fight,
it can grow a new one.

3-4
years

# Adult crab

When a crab reaches adult size,
it is ready to **mate** and
produce young of its own.

# Crab life cycle

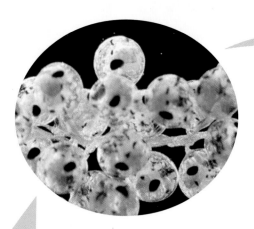

### Eggs
The female produces
thousands of eggs.

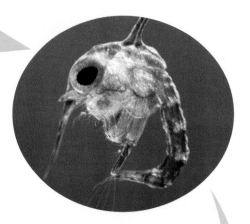

### Larva
The eggs hatch
into tiny **larvae** that
float in the sea.

### Adult crab
A crab reaches its adult size
after three or four years.

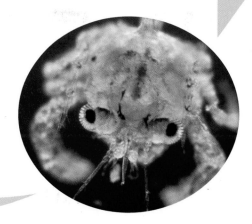

### Baby crab
The larvae **molt** several times,
then become baby crabs.

# Glossary and Further Information

**bristles** stiff hairs

**defend** to protect against attack

**feeler** part of an animal used for touching and smelling

**gills** special part of animal that helps it to breathe under water

**hatch** to come out of an egg

**jointed** made of several parts joined together

**larva** (plural larvae) the tiny, early stage in a crab's life.

**mate** when a male and female come together to produce young

**molt** to cast off an old shell or skin

## Books

**Crab**
by Lloyd G Douglas (Children's Press, 2005)

**What is a Life Cycle?**
by Bobbie Kalman (Crabtree Publishing 1998)

# Index